P9-DSZ-563

This book belongs to

_____

mind power

switch on your sixth sense

mind power

Natalia O'Sullivan
illustrations by Cathy Brear

switch on your sixth sense

RYLAND
PETERS
& SMALL

LONDON NEW YORK

Senior Designer Susan Downing
Senior Editor Clare Double
Production Deborah Wehner
Art Director Gabriella Le Grazie
Publishing Director Alison Starling

Editorial Consultant Christina Rodenbeck

First published in the United States in 2003 by
Ryland Peters & Small, Inc.
519 Broadway, 5th Floor
New York NY 10012
www.rylandpeters.com

ISBN 1 84172 523 4

Printed in China

contents

introduction

This book is written in the belief that everyone has psychic powers, and that these powers are divided into four categories: clairvoyance, clairaudience, clairsentience, and divination. It will introduce you to all aspects of psychic development. You, too, can divine the future, use crystals, meditate, visualize, dream, dowse, and develop your psychic powers. *Mind Power* will show you how to develop your natural intuitive skills—your sixth sense—with just a little encouragement and practice.

Awakening these talents takes time and effort. It is your choice whether or not to develop your latent psychic gifts. The process is similar to learning how to play a musical instrument; first you must have the passion to learn, then patience and discipline before you can become a talented player. To become a psychic you have to want to learn about your gifts and put them to work.

Psychic power is not something only a few people possess. We all have the ability to be psychic; some people are just more awake to their powers than others. The gift of connecting to your psychic potential lies in using your intuitive and psychic senses in life, as part of your everyday personality.

You already have psychic moments, whether it's saying the same thing at the same time as a friend or visiting a place for the first time and feeling that you have been there before. We are aware of the information that we receive through an "inner" sense but often do not talk about it, perhaps for fear that other people will not understand.

To be psychic is to see beyond the physical reality, and to be one step ahead.

how to use this book

Begin with the psychic quiz (pages 12–15). Find out what the different psychic powers are and whether you have a stronger link with one or another. It is best to work on one power at a time and decide which one you enjoy most. Try the solo psychic exercises to develop and strengthen your personal abilities, then play the psychic power games (for two or more people). The solo exercises and games are based on learning, developing, and experimenting with psychic skills. They are grouped by the four psychic powers—you can work with all of them or choose one or two favorites. As long as you follow the guidelines, the games are safe to play with your choice of family members or friends.

what you need

Things you may need to make the most of this book include a pendulum or dowsing tool, crystals, incense, essential oils, oil burner, relaxation tape or music, dream diary, psychic journal, and a favorite pen.

developing your gifts

First ask yourself why you want to practice. You need a reason to exercise your psychic powers, perhaps to improve your concentration or perception. Make the practice a habit; put it in your diary, as you would any other appointment.

- The most propitious starting time is at full moon or new moon.

- Choose your psychic workout.

- Do one practice a week. Return to the first practice at the next full or new moon and observe how much you have improved.

- Document your progress in a "psychic journal." Write a mission statement when you begin the solo workouts, such as "I will achieve the gift of ... by ... " Always state a reward for achieving your goals.

- Finally, work out with a friend. It is sociable, and you are more inclined to stick with your psychic development if you have arranged to meet someone else to practice.

- Don't put off getting started.

practice in your daily life

In addition to doing the exercises in this book, practice using psychic skills daily. Think of something you do every day, such as buying a coffee on the way to work. Resolve to focus your psychic power on this event and then attempt to guess who you will see at the coffee shop and what will happen next, and note any telepathic thoughts or intuitive feelings you had. If you get it right, mark it in your psychic journal. Practicing daily will give you the power to work as a psychic in a grounded and practical manner, as well as improving your skills.

clairvoyance *seeing mentally what is happening in an unseen dimension*

clairsentience *smelling and/or sensing what is unseen*

clairaudience *hearing sounds occurring in an unseen dimension*

divination and spirit communication *opening up to a deeper psychic ability, from simple divination to a more advanced communication with spirits*

the four psychic powers

the psychic quiz

Take this test, then turn the page to discover the nature and extent of your psychic power. Do the quiz every month to see how your abilities are developing. You should see an improvement within a couple of months of starting the solo exercises.

Close your eyes and relax for a couple of minutes. Do you see

A. Nothing?

B. Words and symbols?

C. Colors and shapes?

D. Images and faces?

Ask a friend to imagine a shape. Concentrate and guess what he or she is imagining. Do you

A. Get it completely wrong?

B. Get it right, but don't feel confident to say so and suggest something else?

C. Guess a similar shape?

D. Get it exactly right?

Think of an old friend you haven't spoken to for a while. Make a list of what you think that person has been doing. When you phone your friend, you discover

A. All your guesses were wrong.

B. You were wrong about what your friend had been doing, but right about how he or she had been feeling.

C. At least one of your predictions was right.

D. Several of your thoughts were extremely accurate.

Your partner or best friend has a headache. Do you

A. Offer some aspirin?

B. See that the headache is caused by a buildup of stress, which you sense as heaviness around the person's head?

C. Suggest a natural remedy?

D. Put your healing hands to the person's forehead, which immediately makes him or her feel better?

You visit a friend's house and feel uncomfortable in the atmosphere. Do you

A. Think it is because you are not feeling well?

B. Suggest that there may be a problem in the home, and ask if the people who lived there before your friend had any problems or difficulties?

C. Suggest that your friend changes the decor since it is not enhancing the atmosphere?

D. Think that the place is haunted?

You attend a job interview and take an immediate dislike to someone in the office where you will be working. Do you

A. Think that the person has a seriously negative attitude?

B. Follow your instincts—there is a likelihood that you have a psychic connection with the person, which suggests danger?

C. Find out what the person's role is and make a mental note to avoid him or her?

D. Look into the person's character and find out why you don't like them. Does their star sign clash with yours?

what the psychic quiz tells you

The results of the quiz indicate where your natural psychic abilities lie. Look out for the symbol of each skill by each exercise and game in the book.

If you answered mostly A ...

Your psychic awareness is quite low at the moment, but don't despair. Your answers suggest that you have a logical mind and with practice you will find you have natural clairvoyant skills. You need to let go when working with your psychic powers. A dream diary would be helpful; you'll work with your unconscious mind and bring your latent psychic powers into your daily life. See pages 16–17 for more about clairvoyance.

If you answered mostly B ...

You are very sensitive and naturally clairsentient. You need to trust what you feel about people, places, and situations. Even if you don't always perceive things clearly, you will find that, if you listen to your heart and your gut instincts, your psychic insights will nearly always be accurate. See pages 18–19 for more.

If you answered mostly C ...

It appears that you can hold your own with the most mystical of psychics, but there is always room for improvement. You have clairaudient skills with a touch of mental agility. You need to trust what you sense or hear when you are in challenging situations. You should practice relaxation techniques and meditation to open your imagination and become more susceptible to second sight. See pages 20–21 for more.

If you answered mostly D ...

You've already mastered psychic skills, since you make accurate predictions about people and places. You just need the confidence to know that you can get it right. In particular you have divination skills, but you have the gift to work with the other psychic powers, too. See pages 22–23 for more.

clairvoyance

Clairvoyance is a range of psychic skills based on the ability to have "clear sight or clear vision." Clairvoyants receive information through heightened visual awareness. Their abilities encompass:

Telepathy The ability to tune into the thoughts of others and be able to project their own thoughts into another person's mind.

Visions The ability to interpret symbols and images seen inside and outside people, objects, and places.

Dreams The ability to tune into the higher consciousness while sleeping and bring information back into everyday life by interpreting images seen in dreams.

Precognition/premonitions Knowledge about events before they take place, enabling the clairvoyant to make predictions about the future.

Personality Charismatic, powerful, compassionate, and understanding, with a vivid and creative imagination. Clairvoyants are brilliant at reading people, but may have difficulty perceiving themselves clearly.

Weaknesses Difficulty knowing the difference between physical reality and pure imagination. Clairvoyants lack confidence in their own abilities, may lie or disguise the truth, and can be fearful or over-imaginative.

clairsentience

Clairsentience is the power to sense psychic phenomena that cannot be perceived by any of the five physical senses. Clairsentients have a keen ability to tune into the atmosphere of a place or person. Their abilities encompass:

Psychometry Reading the vibrations of an object or place; reading a person's character and even telling that person's future.

Aura reading Discerning the vibration or color of a person's energy field.

Psychic protection The ability to strengthen, protect, and cleanse their own energy and space; wearing and carrying protective crystals and conducting purification rituals.

Personality Very intuitive and sensitive to others' moods, which can make clairsentients great friends, partners, and lovers.

Weaknesses Over-emotional, self-indulgent, tend to have a "victim" attitude, impressionable, vulnerable to negative psychic energy. If they openly discuss what they sense from people and places, clairsentients can become too open and vulnerable to the expectations of others.

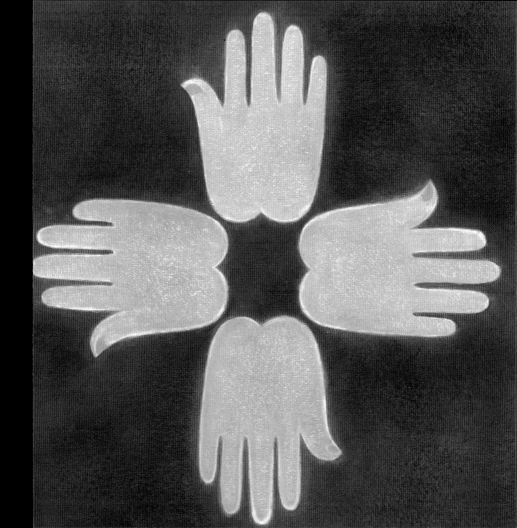

clairaudience

Clairaudience is the ability to hear words or sounds that are not part of the material world but come from the ether and spirit realms. Their abilities encompass:

Hearing Receiving messages from spirit guides.

Listening Tuning into their intuition and higher self. Learning to meditate and still the mind.

Spirit communication Relaying messages seen or felt from the spirit world.

Creativity Expressing psychic power through creativity and communication, including through psychic art and painting.

Personality Clairaudients sense people's thoughts; this is what makes them honest and plain speaking. They take people at face value because they assume everybody else is as straightforward as them. This means that, although they are not exactly gullible, sometimes clairaudients may find it hard to tell when someone is lying

Weaknesses Clairaudients need to learn not to be too afraid of what they hear coming from others' thoughts; they must discern what they wish to hear, as they will be vulnerable to people's subtle demands.

divination

Divination is the ability to see into the future or the past. A diviner's abilities encompass:

Scrying Reading symbols from a bowl of colored water.

Tarot reading Card reading.

Crystal reading Divining using crystals or stones.

Pendulum dowsing Diagnosing and answering simple questions using a pendulum.

Personality A good imagination with a nose for what is real. Diviners are naturally intelligent, instinctive, inquisitive, organized, calculating, and practical. They can translate symbols into a logical structure, and enjoy analyzing people's characters.

Weaknesses Can be self-righteous, demanding, and domineering, expecting too much from life and trying to manipulate the future. Diviners need to learn patience and to relinquish control.

First discover your natural gift by doing the quiz on pages 12–15. You can then choose which psychic workout you want to do first. Begin by practicing the relevant solo exercise for at least seven days and not more than a month. It's best to begin at full or new moon, then continue until you begin to have confidence with the skill to which the exercise relates. You will then be ready to try some of the other psychic workouts.

the psychic workouts

solo exercises

Before you do the solo exercises, you need to make a space at home where you can concentrate, feel comfortable, and won't be interrupted. Whether you choose the tool shed or your bedroom, this space must also be somewhere you feel safe and secure. Make sure it is clean and tidy. Create an uplifting mood by burning your favorite incense or essential oil, lighting a candle, and playing relaxing music. This encourages an atmosphere conducive to successful psychic experience.

Before you can attune yourself to your psychic ability, you must relax. The art of learning to relax in a serene environment in order to still your mind will enable you to release your psychic energies. There are various methods that you can use to unwind, such as yoga, t'ai chi, and relaxation techniques such as the one described below.

• Sit or lie comfortably and close your eyes.

• Slowly and deeply, breathe in and out. Count to seven on the in-breath, hold for three, and breathe out to the count of seven. This teaches your mind to relax and let go.

• Imagine yourself lying on a colorful rug in a beautiful country garden. You are under a tree and a gentle breeze is stroking your face and body.

• Begin to relax your body by feeling the earth on your back and under your head.

• Focus on your feet and keep them as still as you can when you breathe in. As you breathe out imagine any stress and worry leaving your body and sense your feet becoming as light as a feather.

• Next, visualize your legs, knees, and hips. Hold your legs still, breathe in and out, and again sense all your stress and worries leaving your body. Feel your legs becoming as light as a feather. Follow this exercise through your body: your solar plexus, ribcage, shoulders, arms, hands, neck, head, and spine.

• Now simply listen to your body breathing. If any thoughts intrude, gently push them away. Imagine putting them in a suitcase and leaving them by the tree, or putting them in a bubble or huge balloon which then flies into the sky.

• You are now ready to proceed with your psychic workout.

Gather what you need before you start and have your psychic journal and pen ready to write down your experiences and encounters.

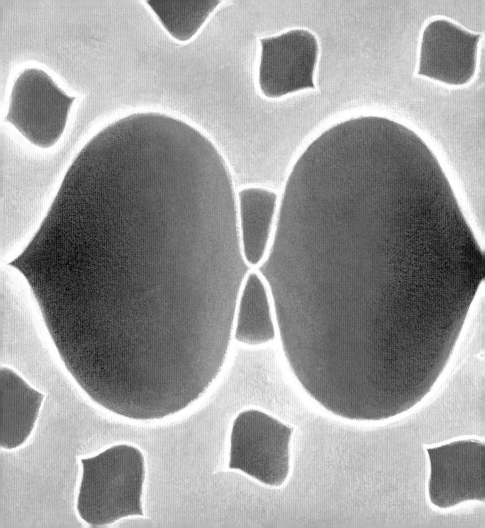

clairvoyance

Opening the third eye

To develop the extraordinary sense of the third eye you will need to learn how to focus your mind's eye and discipline your imagination. This is not as hard as it appears; it just takes concentration and practice.

• Sit in your meditation position, relax and focus on your breathing, then take your attention to the third eye (above your eyebrows).

• Close your eyes and pay close attention to the flow of your thoughts. Simply observing your thoughts will free you from the endless process of creating new ones. In the same way that you can watch your breath, you can watch your mind.

• Observe the thoughts that come to you but do not follow them. If you find that you have slipped and fallen into a stream of thinking, bring your attention back to the third eye and start again.

• Practice this for 10 minutes each day to develop a conscious awareness of your psychic visions.

Visualization is the ritual of focusing your concentration on an image of something you want to create, become, or empower. Many of your thoughts and inspirations will be of a psychic nature, such as visions, prophecies, or glimpses of things happening in other places. For the time being, let these go, focus as an unattached witness.

clairvoyance

dream problem solver

Tools: Pen and paper.

Dreams can be problem solvers. You can go to bed and say a prayer with intent to your inner self. You can find a solution to a problem that you have been worrying about. The problem can be as simple as what to do about something you have lost, or a complex matter such as how best to resolve a health issue.

• If you need to select one problem to focus on out of many, write them all down as a list of questions and work on one at a time.

• Just before you go to sleep, affirm what you have written and place it under your pillow. Try to see the question in picture form rather than words. Once you have set the program running, your dreams should do the rest.

• If you find that you get no answer the first night, present your question over seven nights.

Most dreams are forgotten within 10 minutes of waking. To remember them, run through the dream in your mind before you get up and then write everything down, no matter how unimportant it may seem. Many people find that a dream doesn't mean anything until something happens in their day to remind them of it. Then the answer comes.

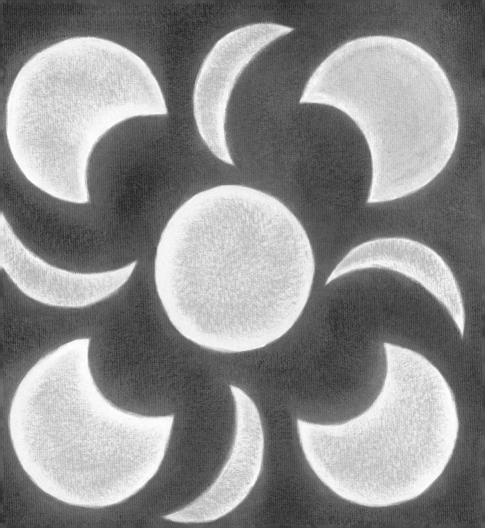

clairsentience

psychic protection

An effective defense against negative feelings and influences is a simple psychic protection exercise. If you ever feel under threat from anyone or anything, you can protect yourself with this visualization technique.

• Get into your favorite relaxation position, whether it's sitting or lying down, and breathe slowly and evenly until you are completely relaxed.

• Imagine a flashlight pointing downwards just above the top of your head. Think about switching on the flashlight and imagine its light shining down on you.

• Let the light cover you entirely so that no part of your body is hidden from it.

• You are now covered in a brilliant white light that offers you spiritual, emotional, and auric protection from negative elements.

• Whenever you feel vulnerable, visualize your shield of light again.

Remember the best protection is a positive attitude and determination. If you have had an argument, feel angry with someone, or just generally negative, avoid any form of divination or psychic activity.

Note: An excellent alternative is wearing a tourmaline crystal pendant; this is a powerful amulet for protecting your psychic energy.

clairsentience

protecting your home

Tools: Sea salt or coarse-grained salt (e.g., kosher salt); lemon, peppermint, or tea tree incense or oil; a pink or purple candle; rosewater, geranium oil, or jasmine oil.

This protection works for areas in the home where you feel negative energy. During this ritual you must ask for guidance and protection from the world of spirits and ask them to help lift the atmosphere.

• Put a small quantity of the salt in a dish and place it in the center of the room. Salt represents Earth, so it will ground your room with calm, benign influences.

• Pass over the dish a lighted incense stick or oil burner containing a protective fragrance such as lemon, peppermint, or tea tree.

• Pass a lighted pink or purple candle over the salt and see the light spiral outwards.

• Blow out the candle, sending light to every corner of the room.

• Finally, to bring a harmonious atmosphere into the room, sprinkle a few drops of rosewater, geranium, or jasmine in each corner.

• Leave the dish in the center of the room until morning, then take the salt outside and bury it, giving thanks to its protective spirit.

Warning: If the atmosphere was created by negative emotions, this practice should clear it. If there is something more sinister at work, you will need an expert.

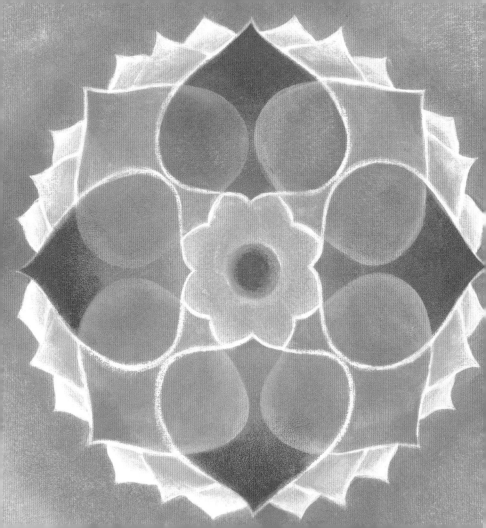

clairaudience

listening to the higher self

Choose a time and place where you won't be interrupted. You need 10 minutes.

• Begin by lying or sitting in a relaxed position. Breathe deeply and slowly to create a cycle of breath (in and out seven times).

• Be aware that your mind is addicted to sound and motion, one thought leading into the next. Observe this and then begin to detach yourself from the mundane: Did I hang out the washing? Did I pay that bill?

• Bring a circle of light down into your mind's eye and see it absorbing all these thoughts. Let it open a space for you so that you can go and sit inside your higher mind. Feel the gentle caress of stillness and peace.

• Now ask to receive a divine force of light. Begin by letting it touch your crown chakra (see page 44). Open it and sense the light coming down through each chakra, reaching down into the base, and spreading itself into the ground.

• Once you feel confident that you can sit like this for more than five minutes, you can ask for visions and inspirations from your higher self. Without trying too hard, you will slowly come to some realizations about yourself and your life, some good and some not so good: the higher self is a realist.

When you come out of this meditation, write down what you have felt and seen. Try keeping a diary of this connection over a period of weeks or months.

clairaudience

herbal crystal bath

Tools: Bath oil or herbs, herbal tea, four candles, a dried sage bundle to burn or an oil burner, and either lavender, geranium, or cedarwood oil, a selection of seven crystals, your favorite relaxing music.

This will help with relaxation and self-awareness.

• Run a bath and add some healing herbs wrapped in cheesecloth or aromatherapy oils to your bathwater. While the bath is running, make your favorite herbal tea.

• Light the candles and burn lavender, geranium, or cedarwood oil in a burner, or burn the sage bundle (only for a few minutes as it will be quite smoky).

• Get into the bath and place the crystals you want to work with on each of your seven chakras (see page 44), or you can place the crystals on your belly, around your shoulders, under your feet, or at base of your spine—whichever part of your body is tense and needs healing or opening up.

• Invite the energies of the stones to work with you for inspiration. You can also seek to be healed and relaxed inside your mind and body.

• Close your eyes and let yourself drift off. Give yourself at least an hour of luxuriating in your bath. Play music or have complete silence.

When you have finished, write down or record your experience.

divination
scrying crystal water

Tools: Two white candles, glass or crystal bowl of water, quartz or amethyst crystal.

• Make a list of questions that you wish to divine. Be realistic.

• Place the two candles either side of the bowl of water. Make sure the flames don't reflect in the water. Put the crystal in the center of the bowl.

• Call upon your guiding powers to assist you.

• Relax with a cycle of seven breaths. Close your eyes and say, "My mind is clear, my vision pure." This will help you achieve a non-judgmental state in which to see.

• Let your eyes drift out of focus as you gaze into the water. Gradually you'll see images and shapes. Suddenly you will no longer know if your eyes are open or shut.

• Often there are three sets of images: the present, the underlying influences, and the way forward or action. Roughly, an image moving towards you means an event will occur soon; moving away means an event or person is moving away, or a past influence or relationship still affects you; to the left, physical occurrences; to the right is symbolic; center or top are important and need immediate attention; at the bottom are less urgent. The size of images can indicate their importance.

Warning: It's easy to become an addict! If you don't like the results of a reading, don't rush to do another. Be selective and use this skill when you really need clarity.

divination

seeing your aura

All living things have an aura that can be seen or sensed by psychics. It is an egg-shaped band of beautiful vibrant rainbow colors around the physical body. The colors of the aura reflect our physical, emotional, mental, and spiritual states. The best time to do this is in the evening and the best place is a room where you will not be disturbed, preferably your bedroom, where you can lie down.

• Focus on your breath and breathe slowly until your body is relaxed.

• Turn off main lights so that only a small amount of light filters through the window, or from the hall or landing.

• Hold your hands straight out in front of you. Look gently but do not stare. Try fixing your attention on your hands while focusing on the wall. This will help you get the sense of the way to look, to see your aura.

• Bring the fingertips of each hand towards each other until they are close but not touching. The aura should appear as fine lines of light and if you are lucky, shades of color.

• Try rubbing your hands together, which opens up the energy flow.

The most common auric colors are red, orange, yellow, green, blue, violet, white, gold, and silver.

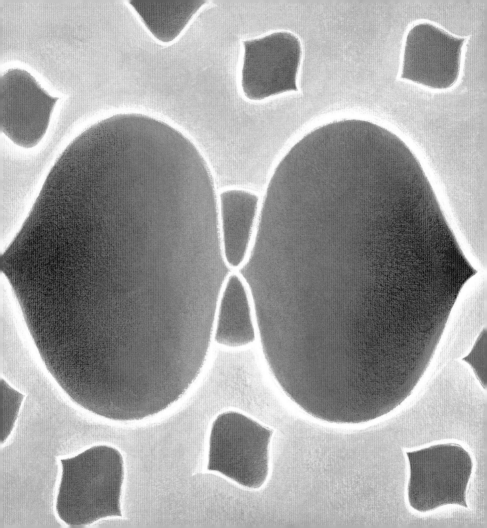

chakra meditations

Chakras are colored wheels of energy in your body that connect the physical and spirit worlds. Each is the center for a particular power, so being in tune with your chakras is essential to finding your own psychic potential. During these meditations you may want to focus on the illustration of the chakra in this book. When you complete a meditation, repeat twice more, then return to your natural breath. Keep still for a few minutes so the effect integrates into your psychic system. Close down.

chakra	power	location in body	colour	illustration
base	sexual	base of the spine	red	page 35
sacral	emotional	below the navel	orange	page 39
solar plexus	material	navel	yellow	page 32
heart	love	chest	green	page 54
throat	communication	larynx	blue	page 50
third eye	visual	forehead	indigo	page 28
crown	spiritual	top of the head	white	page 36

Base Take a deep breath through your nose into your belly. On a slow out-breath, express "Aaahh." Focus on the base chakra and contract your anal sphincter as strongly as possible. Relax on the next inhalation.

Sacral Breathe sharply through your mouth into your chest. Hold briefly, then let the breath fall into your lower belly. Exhale firmly through your mouth and chant "Sol." Breathe in, focus on the chakra, then relax.

Solar plexus Breathe sharply through your nose into your chest. Hold briefly; let the breath fall into your upper belly. Breathe out firmly through your mouth. On your next exhalation chant "Sum." Inhale focusing on the solar plexus. Exhale, relax.

Heart Breathe slowly through your nose into your belly. Hold, lift the breath into your chest three times, and let it fall back. Exhale through your mouth. On the next exhalation chant "Eeee." Inhale, focus on the chakra, exhale, and relax.

Throat With your belly muscles suck your breath through your mouth seven times. Push it out seven times the same way. Next inhale deeply and on the exhalation chant "Uuuu." Focus on the throat chakra, and with your next exhalation, relax.

Third eye Put the middle finger of your right hand on your third eye and the thumb on your right nostril. Breathe slowly into your belly through the left nostril. Close it with your ring finger and hold for four seconds, then breathe out through your right nostril. Do the same on the other side. Repeat each side seven times. Finish with a deep inhalation. Chant "Sunn" as you exhale. Focus on the third eye, relax.

Crown Breathe through your nose into your belly; hold for 12 seconds. Breathe out through your mouth; hold for 12 seconds. Inhale through your mouth. Exhale; inhale deeply. Exhale chanting "Auum." Focus on the chakra, breathe, relax.

games

Before you play the games, try to choose fellow players who are like-minded and have an interest in psychic development. Test them with the psychic quiz to ensure that they are suitable to join you. Make it an exclusive club!

Play the games a few times with people you know well. This will help you understand the principles behind them. Be flexible with the results. The more you play, the better you'll become. Always practice somewhere safe and comfortable.

• Before you begin a game, make sure the room has a good atmosphere (see page 26) and you have everything you need.

• Lead everyone through a relaxation technique and, when you have finished the game, close everyone down (see page 62).

• When people arrive, get them to write down their names and details in your journal and when they leave, ask them for feedback. This will encourage you to test your abilities and be a biographer of any supernatural events.

• When dealing with any difficult characters, do the psychic protection exercise (see page 33) after they have left.

• Remember that practice makes perfect!

Every time you play the games, it should be fun, exciting, even a revelation.

psychic tips

• Keep a dream diary by your bed and write down any vivid dreams.

• Learn to understand psychic symbols in life to help with premonitions, clairvoyance, and divination skills.

• Keep a telepathic thoughts diary to record your accuracy.

• Meditate for five minutes a day to learn how to empty your mind of thoughts. This encourages clear psychic perception.

clairvoyance

guru and the psychic twins

Tools: Quotations or sayings written on slips of paper. They should be brief and easy to capture in an image.   *Players: 7, 9, 11, or 13.*

• Collectively appoint a Guru. Everyone else pairs up by picking names out of a hat.

• The Guru selects one pair of players to be the first "psychic twins."

• The twins choose a quotation and leave the room to decide how they are going to project an image to represent the quote.

• Meanwhile, the rest of the group sits in a circle and closes their eyes. The Guru talks the group into a relaxation meditation, focusing on the color purple and centering concentration on the third eye (see page 29).

• The twins return and sit in the circle. The Guru asks the group to open their eyes.

• For five minutes the twins project the image by telepathy. Their eyes must be open to project clearly. Collectively the group opens its mind to receive a message.

• Afterwards, the group may question the twins for up to 10 minutes.

• Each pair quietly decides what the quotation could be and writes their answers and names on a piece of paper, which they give to the Guru.

• The Guru chooses another pair of twins and the game is repeated.

At the end of the evening the Guru announces the best senders and receivers.

clairvoyance

sending a telepathic image

Tools: A book.   Players: Two.

• Decide who will be the receiver and who the sender.

• Sit opposite each other.

• If you are the sender, select a single word from the book. Create an image in your mind that symbolizes the word.

• Both sit comfortably, relax, and focus on your breathing. Then take your attention to the third eye (see page 29).

• The sender holds the image for five minutes, then projects it to the receiver, who should open his or her mind to receive it.

• After five minutes, find out if the receiver saw anything. Discuss the accuracy of the image: at first you may get only the color or shape.

Then swap roles. Practice with the same person over a few days. Try sending an emotion with an image; emotions are much easier to perceive psychically.

clairsentience

mystery objects

Tools: Small objects personal to someone your fellow player doesn't know, perhaps family heirlooms.   Players: Two.

• Ask a friend to bring a mystery object and do the same for him or her. Exchange objects.

• Hold your object in the palm of your hand. Touch it all the way around, until you begin to sense an energy or a feeling.

• Start to talk about what you see or feel. Say everything that comes into your head, then begin to put it in a coherent order. The impressions that you can pick up from psychometry are limitless. Always express what you see as practically as possible, for the benefit of the other person.

• Talk about the character and appearance of the object's owner.

• Next, focus on the person's past: childhood, relationships, family, and so on. Then move forward in time, picking up the person's current profession and relationships. Keep going until you reach the present, describe events that have recently happened; his or her car, home, profession, and family life.

• Next, you may see symbols: images that appear not to have any physical relevance. Try to relate these to the person's life.

Discuss what you have discovered and make a note in your psychic journal.

clairsentience

the psychometry game

Tools: Each player should bring three pieces of jewelry or small artefacts they've had for a long time. Lidded box, notepad, pens, envelopes.   Players: Two, four, or six.

• Create a comfortable, secure, and peaceful space. Ask each person to write a brief autobiography to test the authenticity of the reading. Put each in an envelope.

• Have half the group (the readers) leave the room and the rest (the receivers) each place one of their items in the lidded box.

• The box is put in the center of the room and the receivers sit in a semicircle. One reader at a time takes an item out of the box and names its owner. Most people have to guess at this point; it doesn't matter if you get it wrong.

• Pair one reader with one receiver. It is time for the readers to describe the objects in more detail. Follow the instructions in the Mystery Objects Game (see page 52). The receiver can participate but not give too much information away.

• The receiver will offer the other receivers' items to the reader while continuing with the reading.

• Each reader has 20 minutes to give a psychometric reading. Then swap roles.

• At the end, write down your findings and check the biographical information in the envelopes. The person who was the most perceptive gets a prize.

• Close down your psychic energy afterwards and use psychic protection (page 33).

clairaudience

psychic art

Tools: Art materials of your choice.   *Players: Two.*

• Invite a friend to sit for you to draw or paint.

• Visualize someone standing next to him or her. You may see the whole person or one feature. Some people cannot see anyone until the picture unfolds on the paper. This may be no more than an outline of light or shade that you trace over.

• Let your pen, pencil, or chalk guide you.

• As you begin to draw, you may find yourself knowing details about the life of the spirit whose image is appearing. Use a tape recorder or ask the person you are tuning into to write down any details that you pick up.

• You may have drawn a spirit guide, or linked into the psyche of the other person and picked up his or her memory of a deceased relative or friend.

• The person you are tuning into may recognize the spirit from dreams or may be aware of a presence that has been with him or her for a long time.

• A sitter who does not recognize the picture can take it home and ask friends or relatives. Sometimes the subject is someone who will be significant in the future.

clairaudience

meet your spirit guide

Important: Read the warnings on pages 62–63 before undertaking this exercise.

Tools: Candles, incense.   Players: Six.   Time: Full moon.

• Do this in a darkened quiet room. The group should relax and concentrate, breathing slowly and letting go of the mind's flotsam. Wait until the atmosphere feels right. Read a prayer or saying from your favorite book, then ask everyone to close their eyes and call upon the divine spirit to bring in all your guides.

• Follow the rhythm of your breath. As you dissolve into pure relaxation, you should begin to feel the love and healing energy of your spirit guide.

• Build up a picture in your mind of the way the guide looks. Try to "hear" a voice with its special accent. Question your own guide, aloud or silently.

• Once you have meditated on your guides, sit in pairs opposite each other. Hold hands and take it in turns to give a message from your spirit guide to your partner.

• Say whatever comes into your head, or talk about any strong feelings you have about your guide. You may see things about their lives or just a spiritual message.

• Change pairs until the whole group has spoken to each other.

At the end of the ceremony close down (see page 62) and ask the spirit world to guide and protect you in the real world.

divination

auric spin the bottle

Tools: Bottle, pendulum.   *Players: Four or more (must be an even number).*

• Sit in a circle. To choose who is to be read, spin the bottle. That person should sit in the center of the circle.

• Spin the bottle to choose one person to be the clairvoyant, one the clairsentient, and one to divine. They should sit three to four feet apart.

• Readers prepare by deep breathing and closing their eyes. Ask permission to proceed and request that the auric body be revealed to you all.

• The clairvoyant stays sitting and uses only his or her vision.

• The clairsentient feels the aura with his or her hands.

• The diviner uses the pendulum to dowse the aura (see page 45).

• Complete this exercise after 15 minutes.

• Each reader gives an individual interpretation and diagnosis of the condition and state of the aura.

• Separate yourself from the person being read by imagining a safety curtain of light coming down between you and that person.

Repeat the game with another member of the group and swap roles.

warnings

Never underestimate the strong effects psychic power has on your mind, body, and spirit.

If you find that you are becoming overwhelmed, you may be receiving too much from the practices. You may not be ready to work with your psychic powers. If you ever experience strong emotions, uncontrolled anxiety, or a sense of being ungrounded after any practice, work more slowly or stop altogether. Your intuition should tell you when you can start again.

closing down

It is essential that you close down after each psychic workout. This ensures that you ground and protect your personal psychic and spiritual energy.

• Visualize each of the chakras (see page 44) as a flowerhead that opens and closes.

• Begin to close down from the crown and work down to the root.

• See each center close down, either as a flower with all its petals slowly furling or as a door closing.

• Be aware that your own energy will still pass in and out as the flower breathes, but your central core is completely protected.

working with spirit communication

Accepting a spirit guide does not mean that you give up your autonomy. Guides are there only to advise; they cannot and do not make choices or force you to accept theirs. The majority of guides interact with you in a friendly, benevolent manner. Always trust your instincts; if you are unhappy with a spirit who has come to work with you, ask the spirit not to come to you again. Protect yourself.

becoming a professional

If you have spent time learning how to use all the practices and games in this book and you find that certain psychic powers are becoming acutely developed, this is the time to decide whether you wish to become a professional. Before you do, please enrol on a psychic development course at an affiliated college or faculty. There is a world of difference between practicing on family and friends, and working with clients. Never begin a professional practice without appropriate qualifications and insurance.

index